A Little Piece of Seoul

Jaein Kim

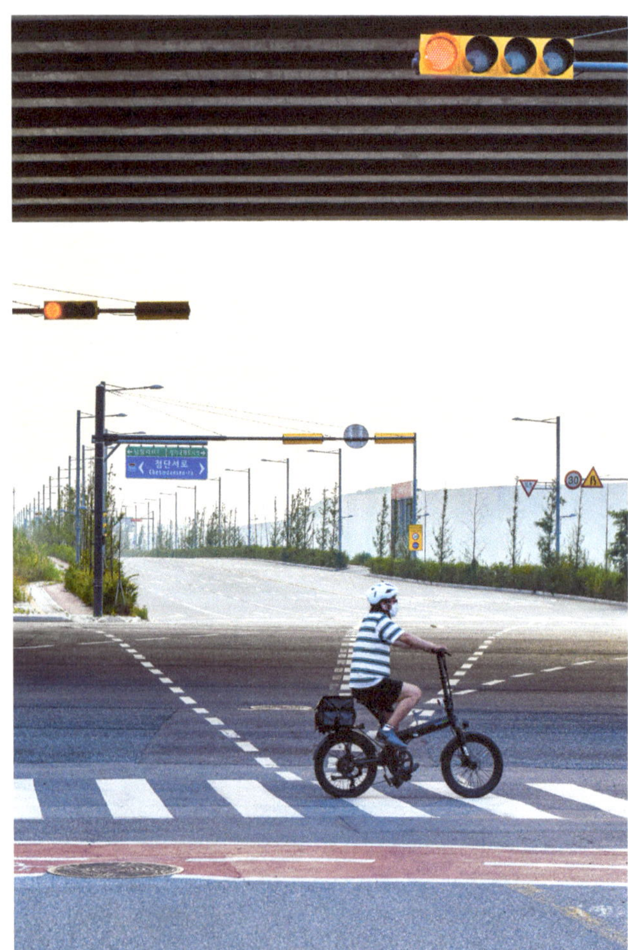
청단서로
30

Born in Place A, but lives in Place B.
Which of the two is "home?"

It may be a matter of legal technicalities,
job or family location,
or whereever one simply desires to be.
Frankly straightforward, my answer is that
I don't know.

Seoul, South Korea is my "Place A,"
yet my "Place B" exists elsewhere.
In Place A, I comfortably stand my place
as a familiar foreigner.

Foreign, in that I see all the strange new changes in one go. That culturally I'm missing a piece or two. Familiar, in that I hold memories of what was there before. That this is my alpha, where my roots are planted.

Yet Seoul is still foreign enough that I feel like a tourist at times. Every alley and every street seems to hold something interesting: things I probably wouldn't see if this is where my timeline of "today" stands.

And I'd like to believe
there's a certain amount of artistic power in that.
So allow me to show you a glimpse
of what I remember as home,
a little piece of Seoul.

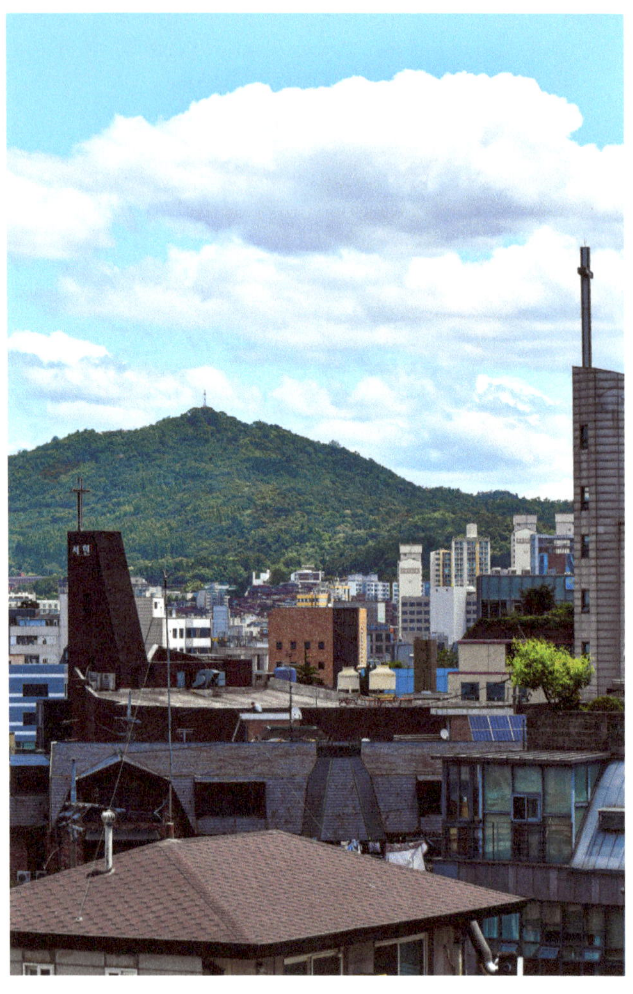

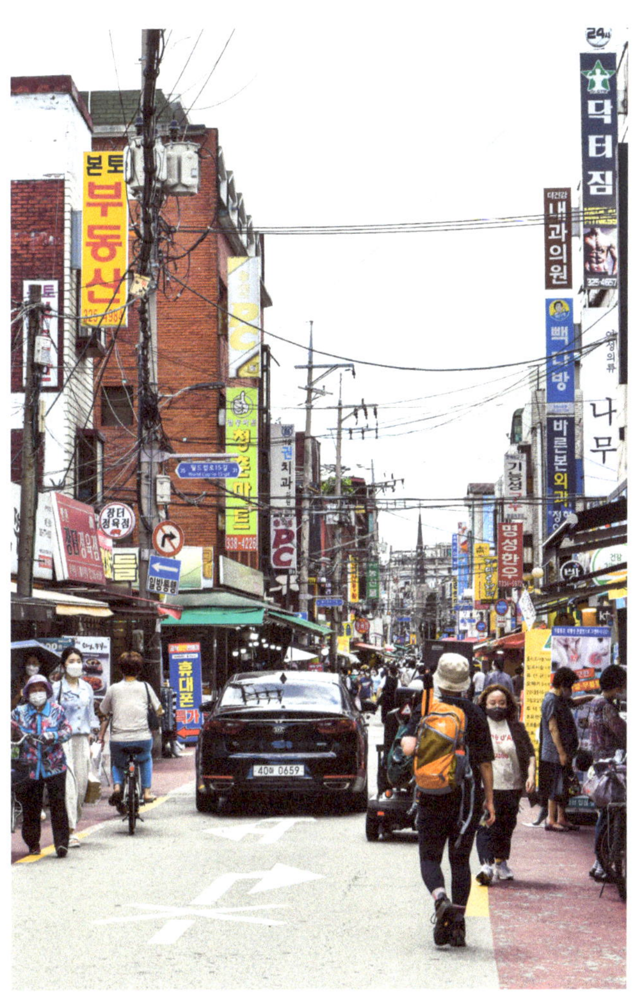
본토
부동산
닥터짐
내과의원
빽다방
나무
청춘마트
치과
장터
정육점
일방통행
명성한우
휴대폰

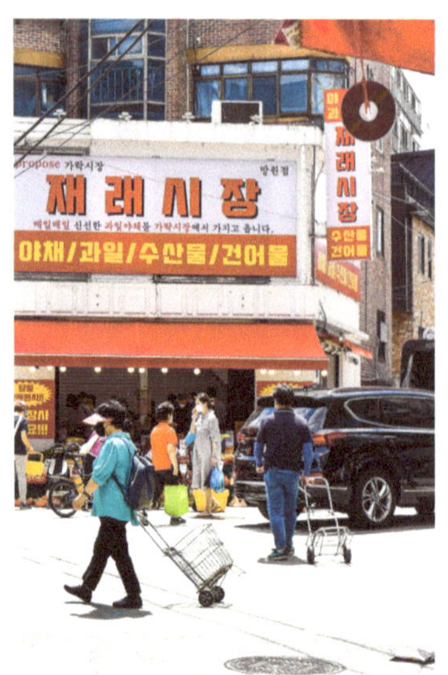
propose 가락시장
망원점
재래시장
매일매일 신선한 과일야채를 가락시장에서 가지고 옵니다.
야채/과일/수산물/건어물
재래시장
수산물
건어물

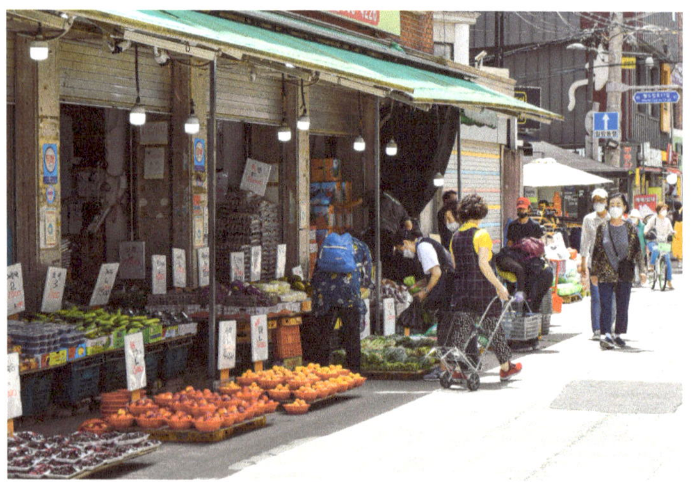

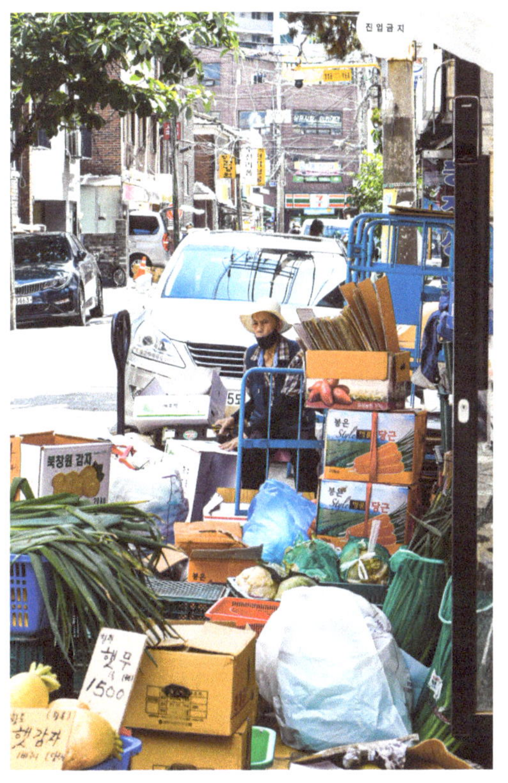
진입금지
북창원 감자
봉은
Style
당근
햇무
1500
햇감자

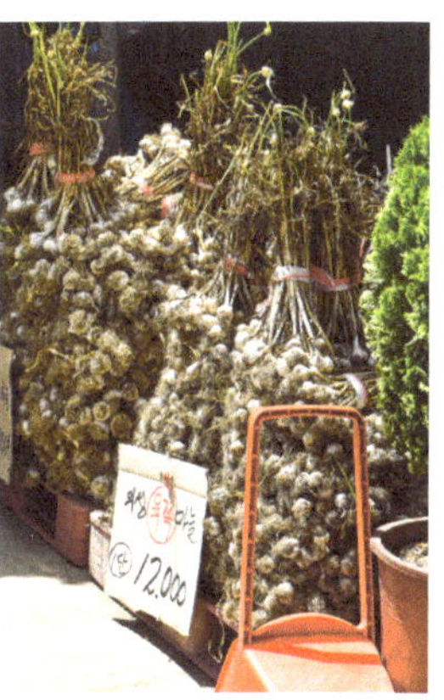
12,000

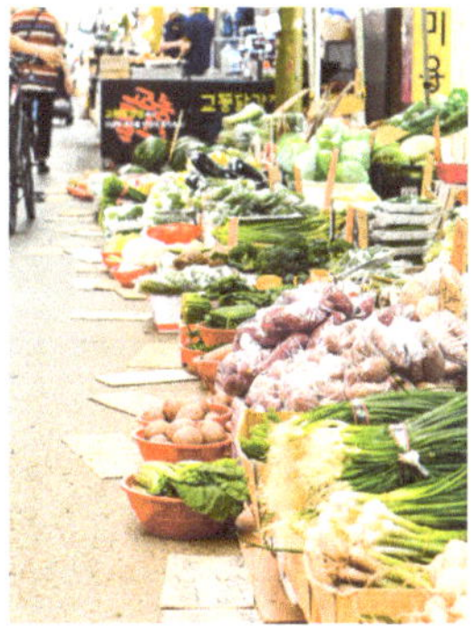

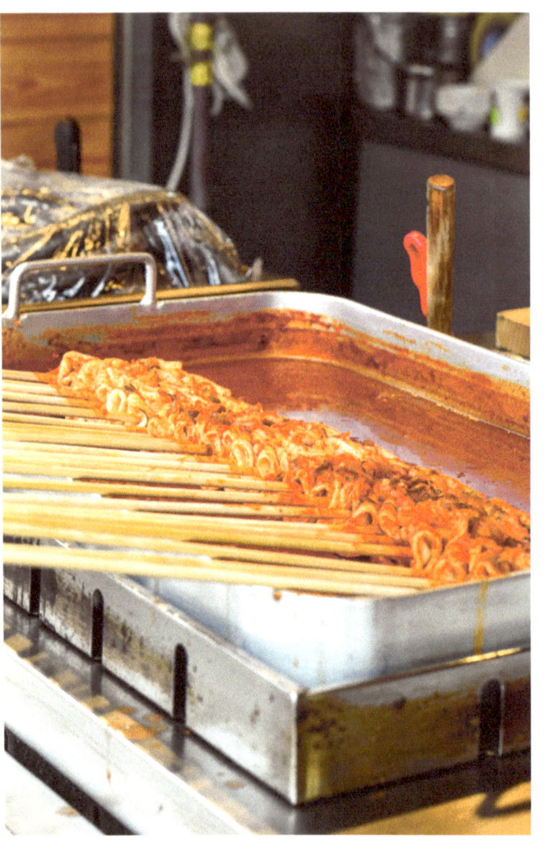

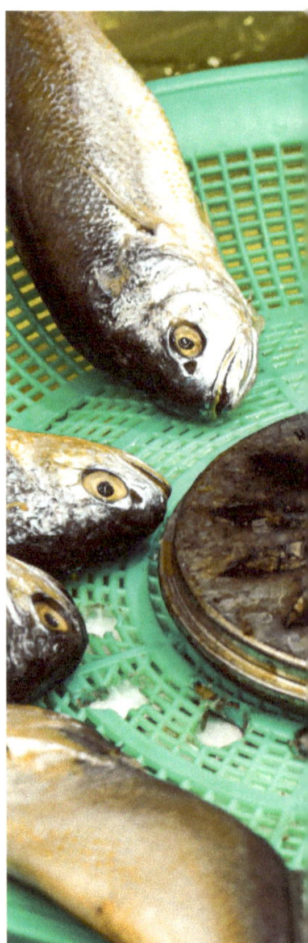

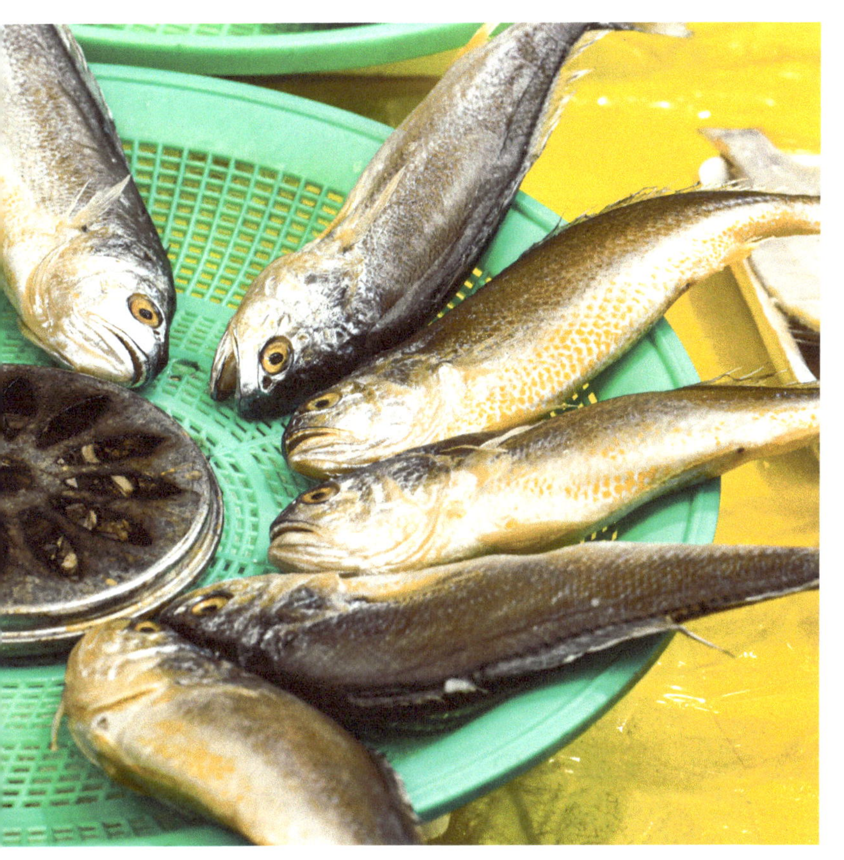

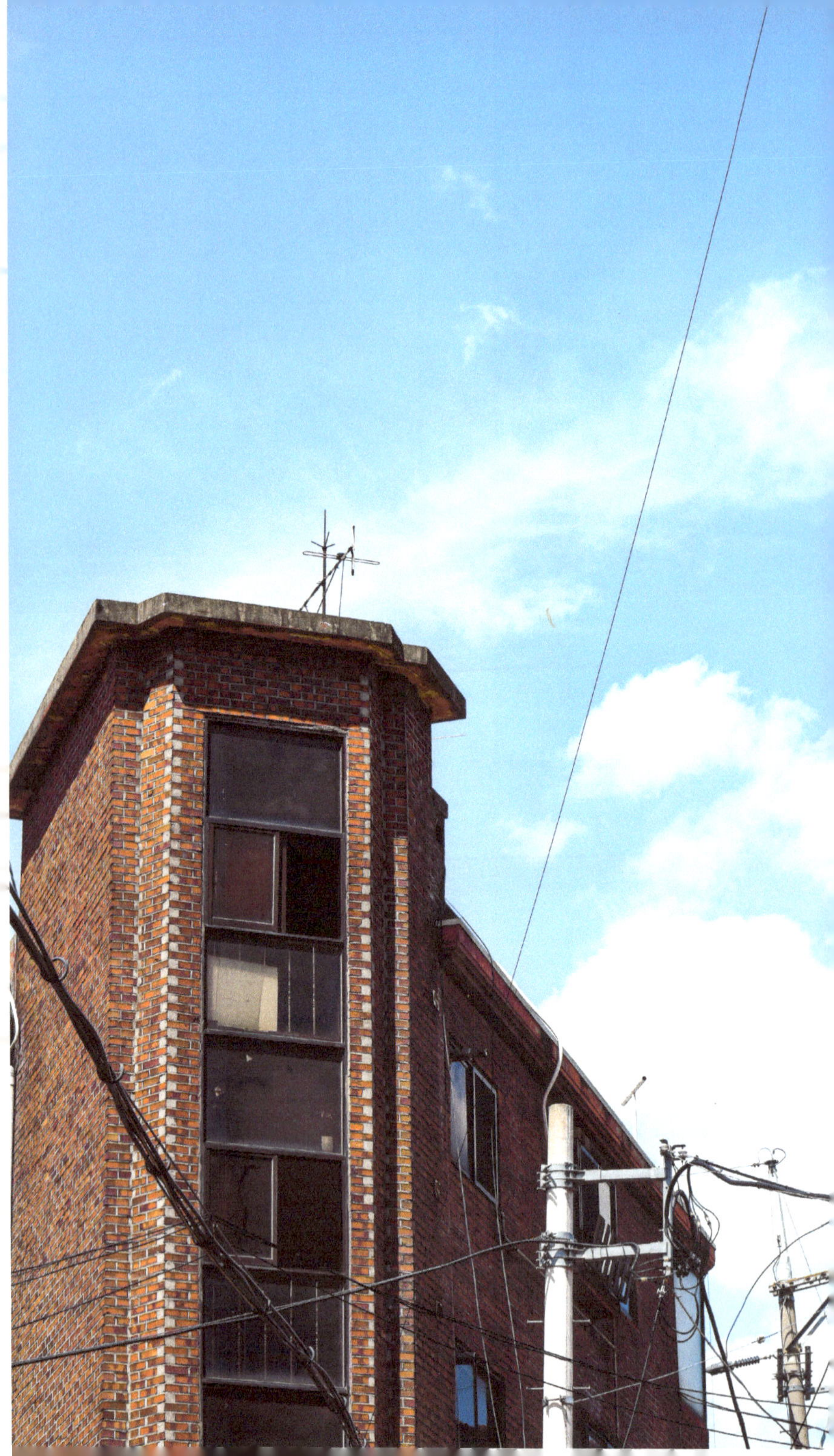

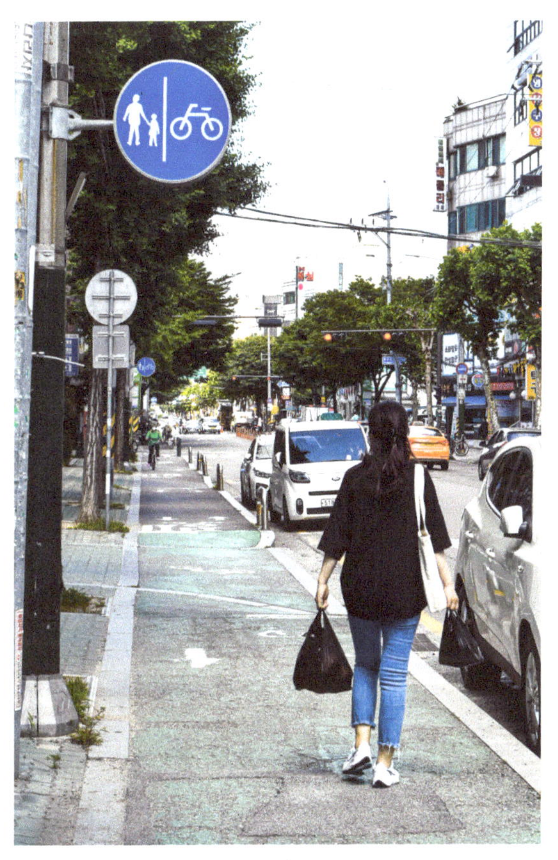

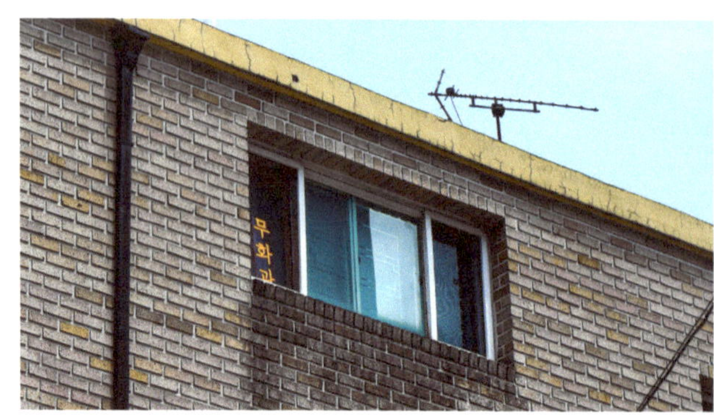
무화과

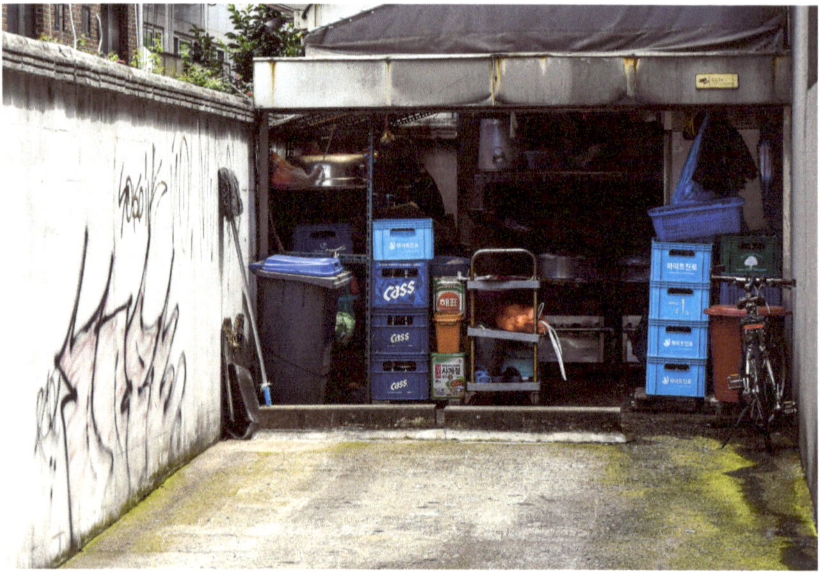

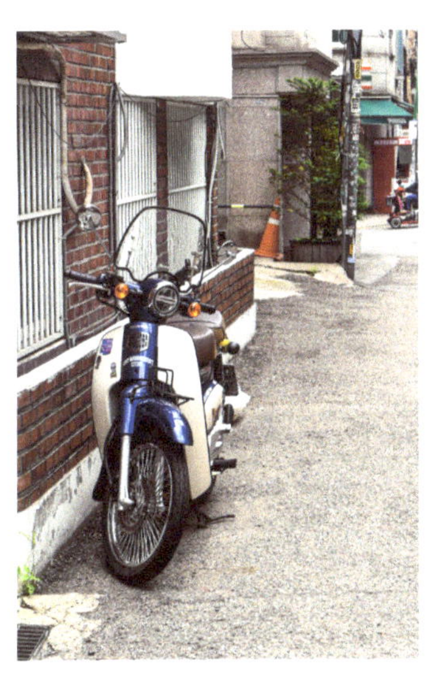

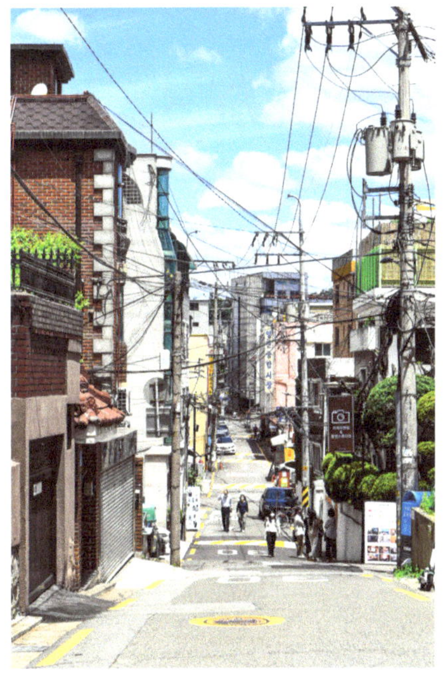

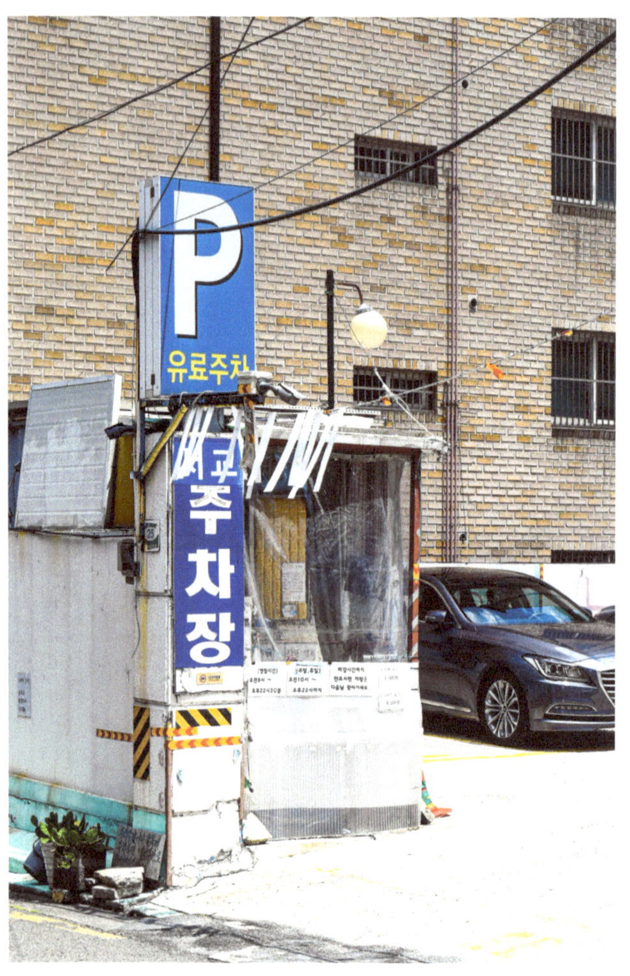
P
유료주차
주
차
장

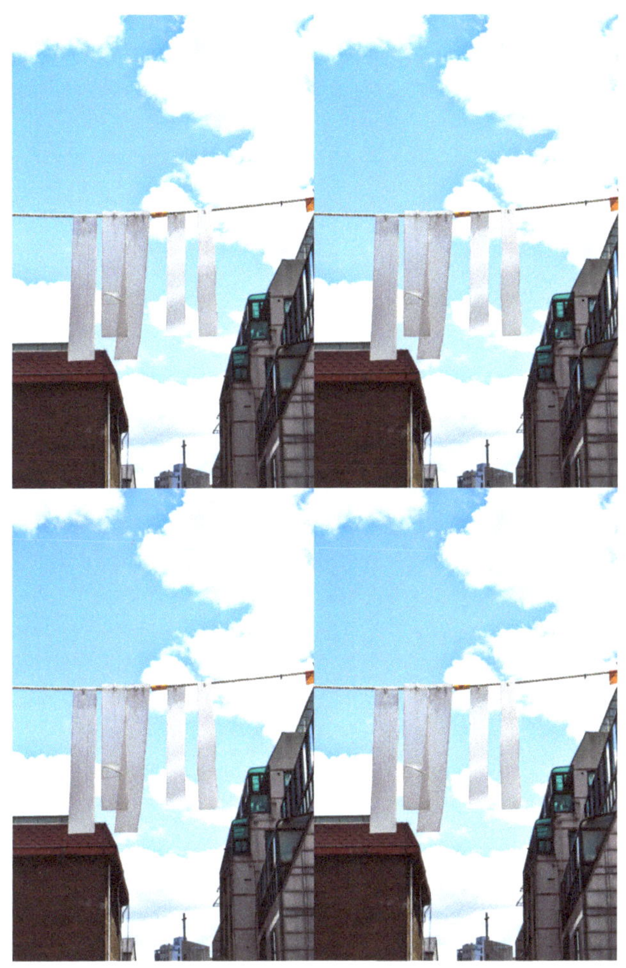

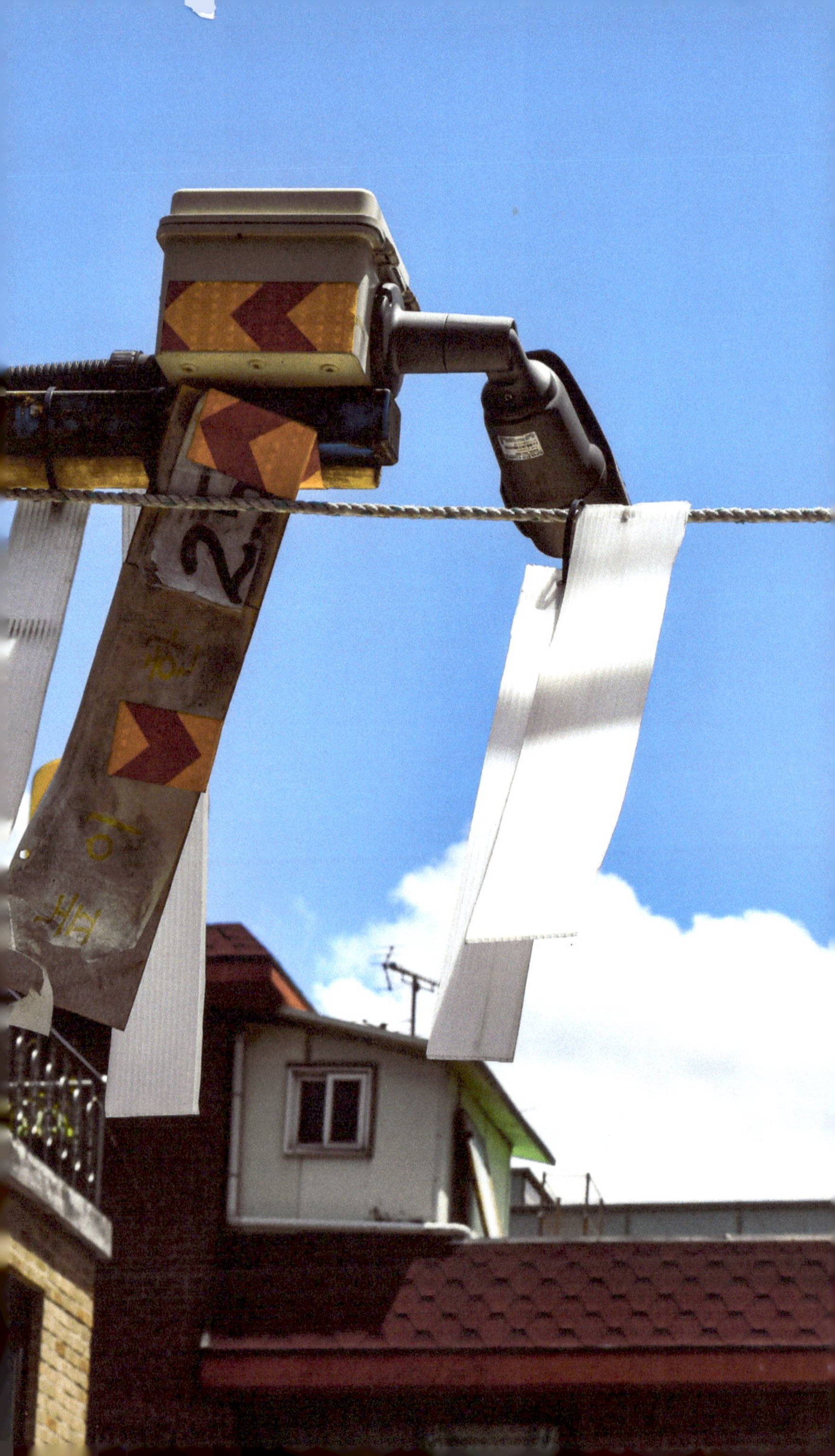

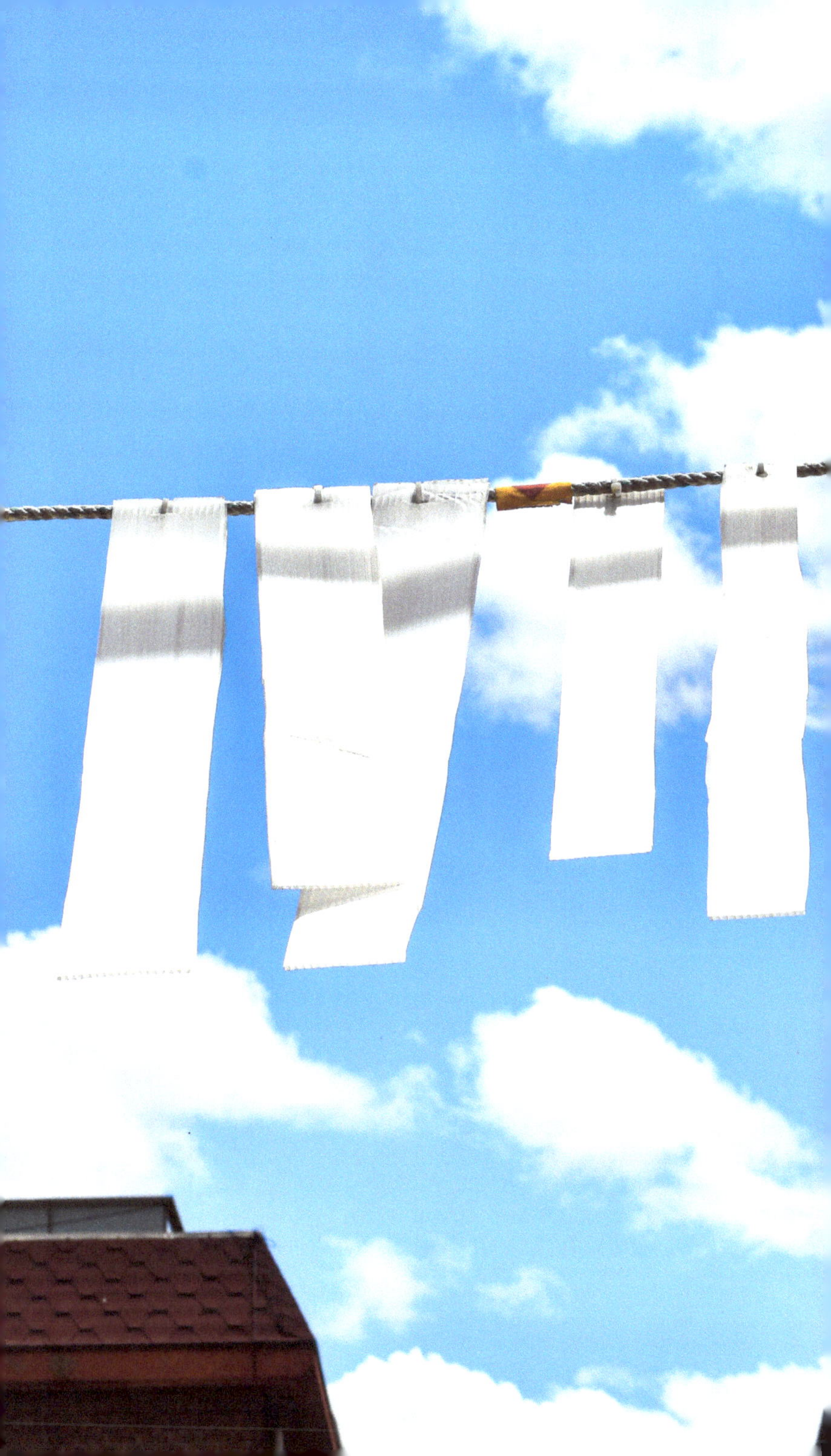

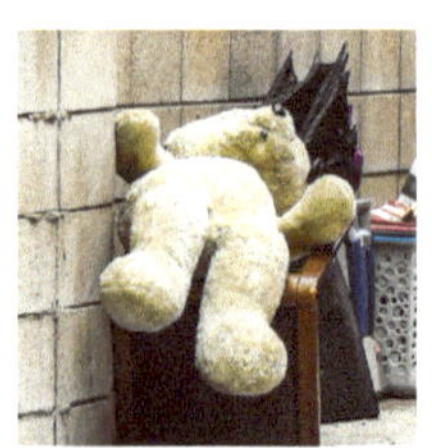

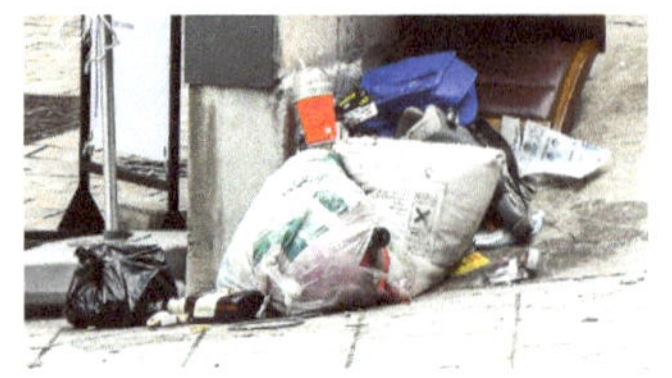

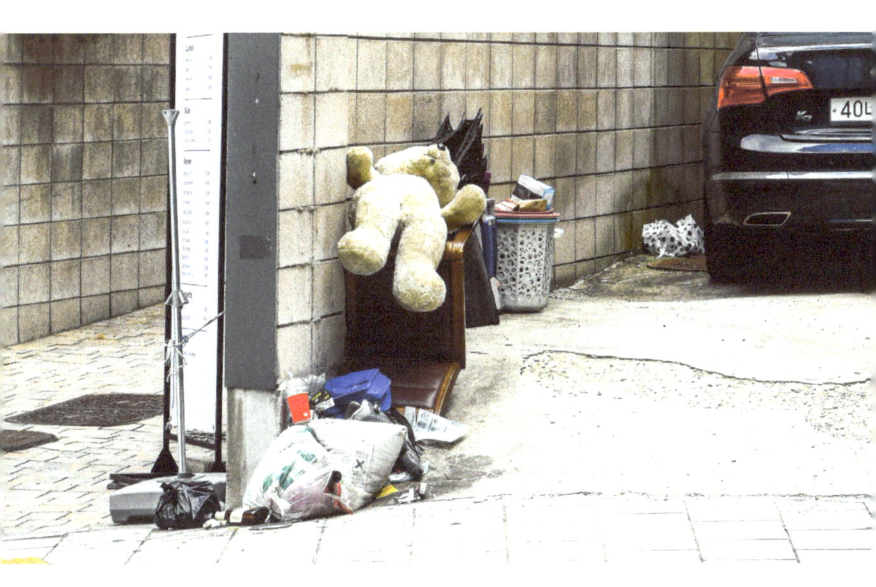

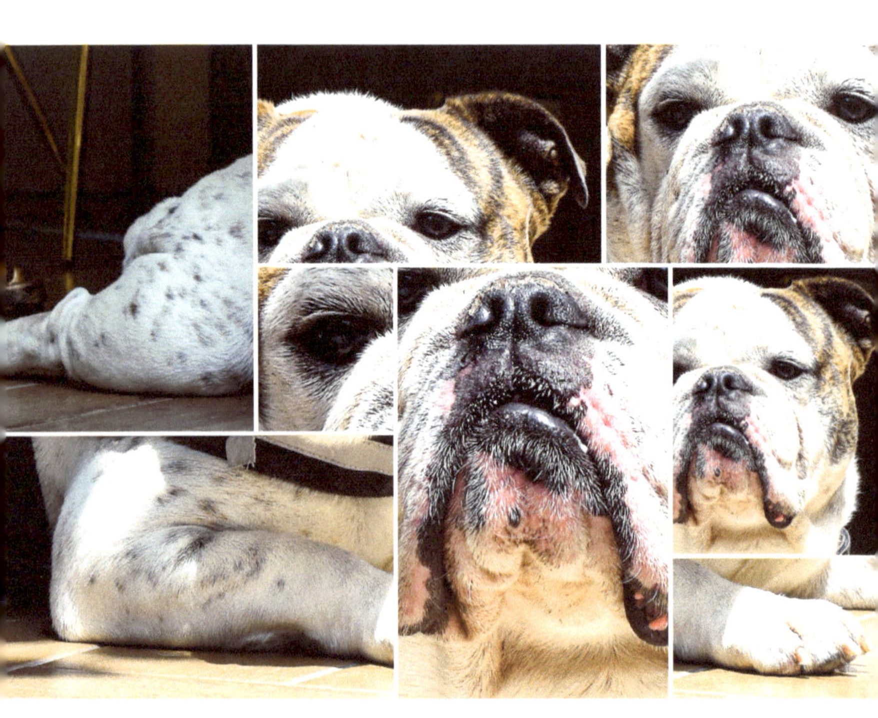

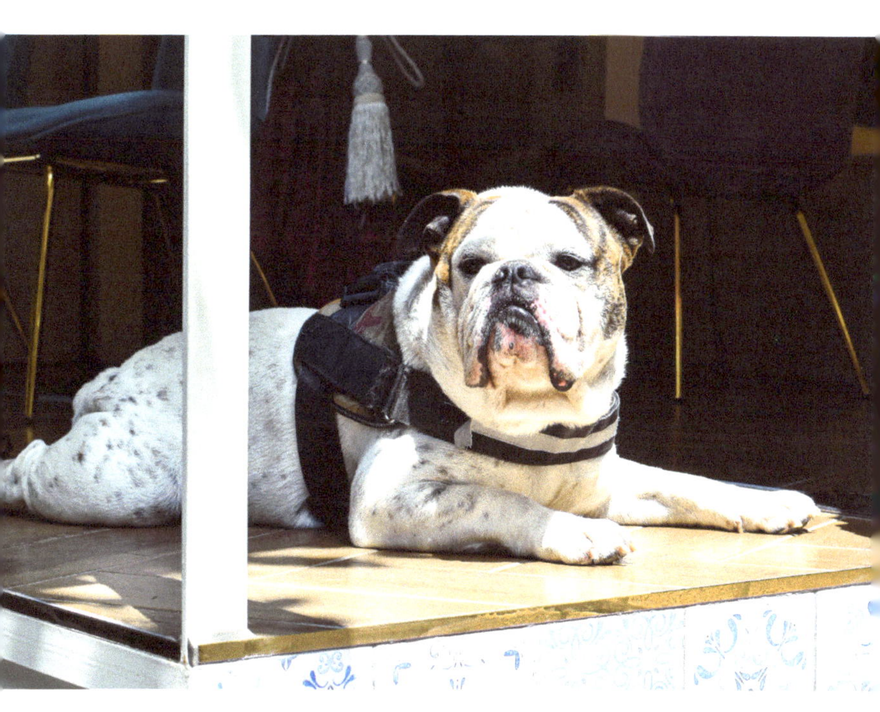

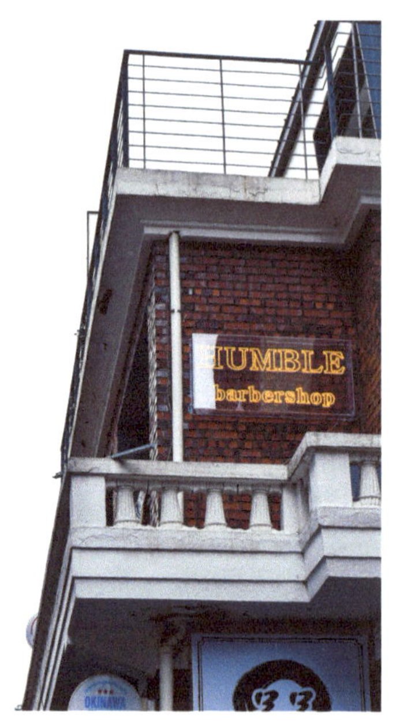
HUMBLE
barbershop
OKINAWA

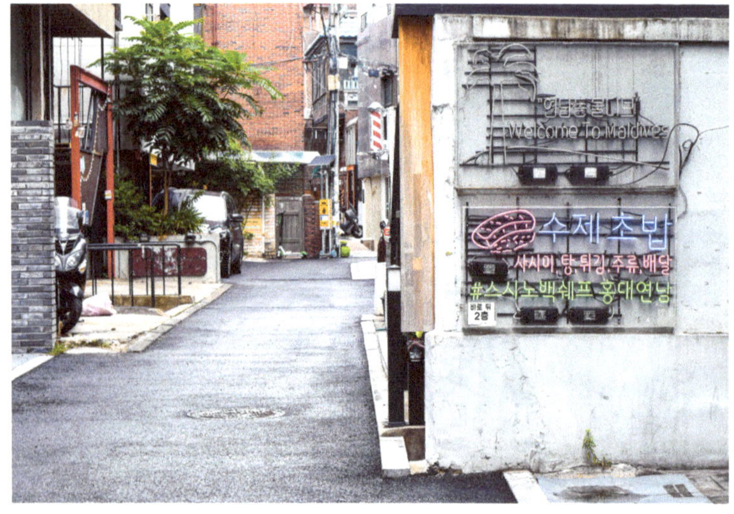
Welcome To Maldives
수제초밥
사시미, 탕, 튀김, 주류, 배달
#스시노백쉐프 홍대연남
바로 뒤
2층

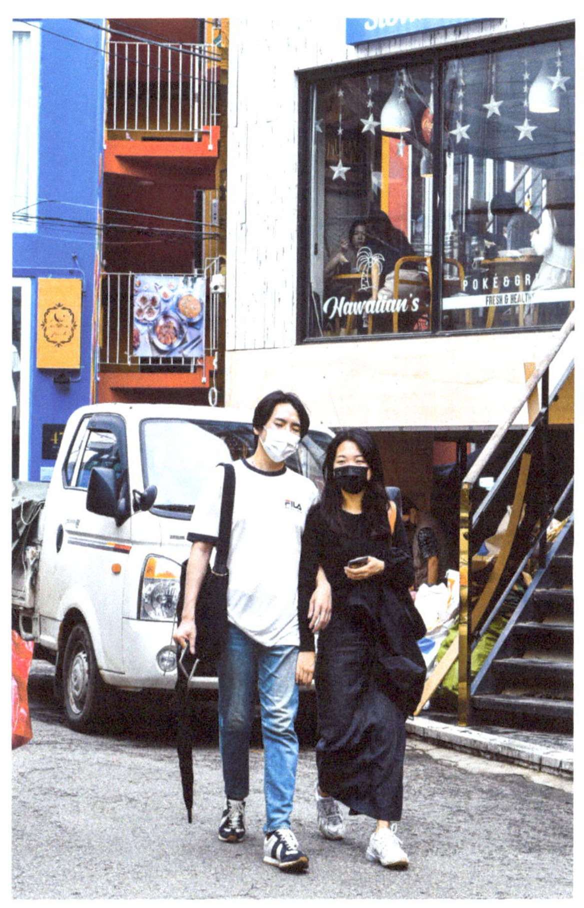
Hawaiian's
FILA

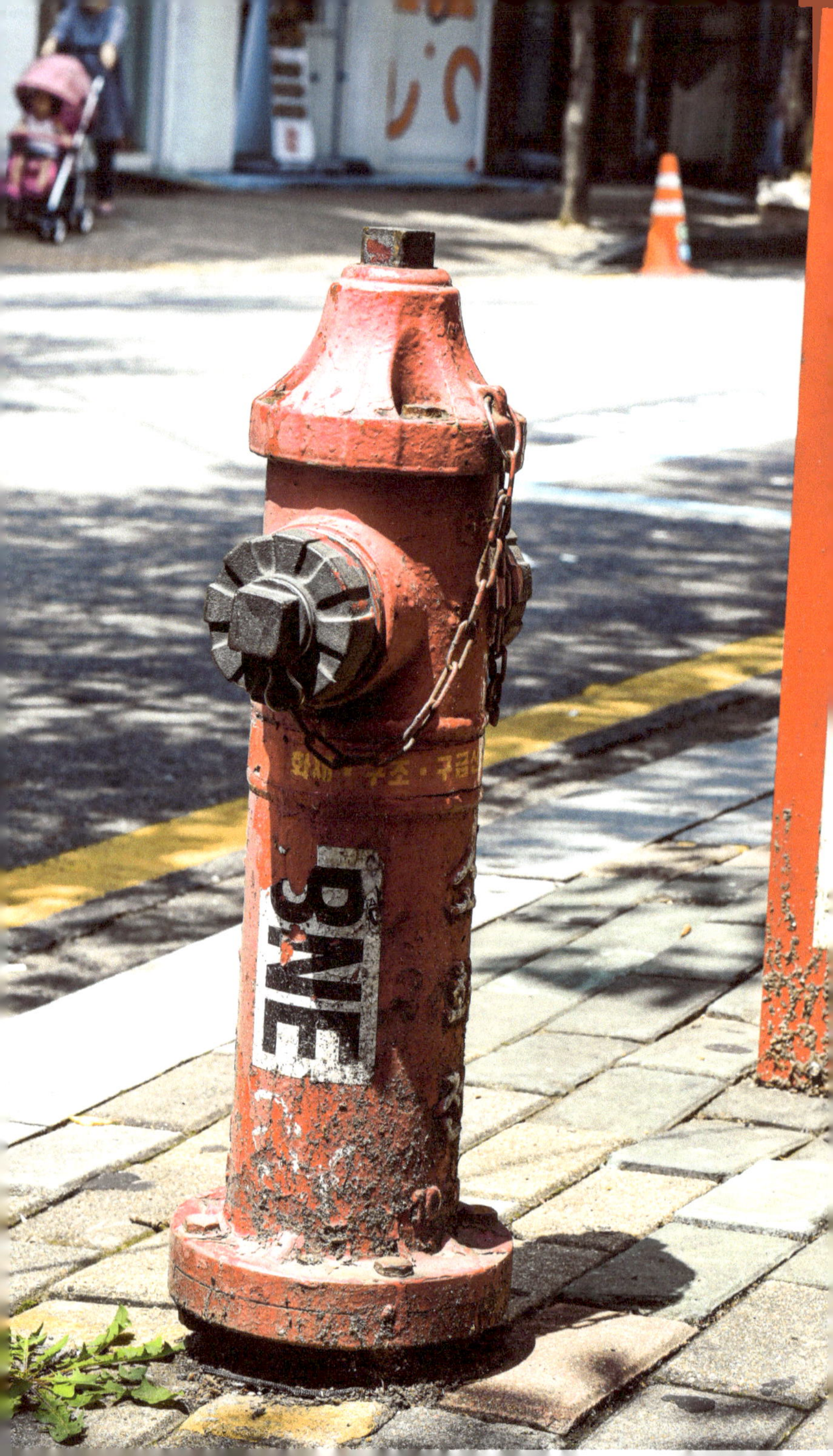

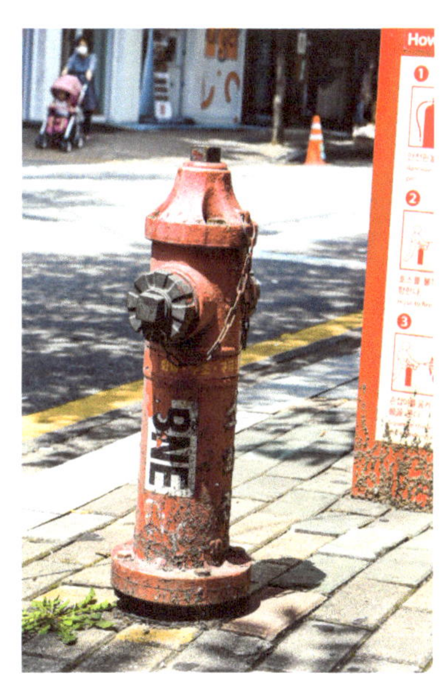

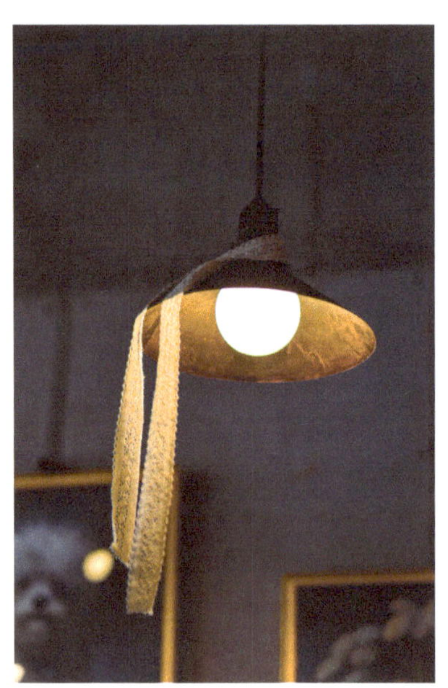

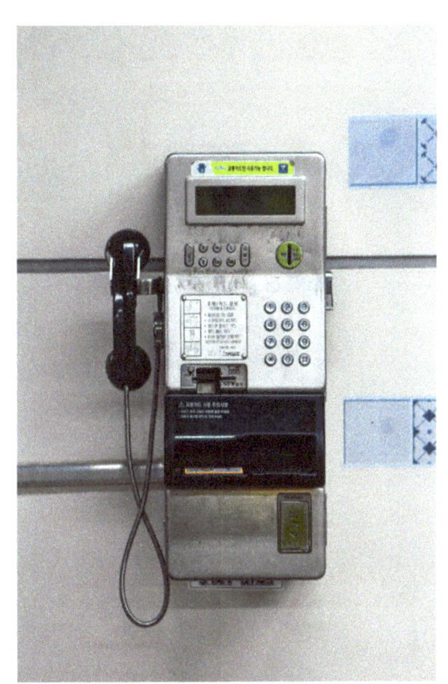

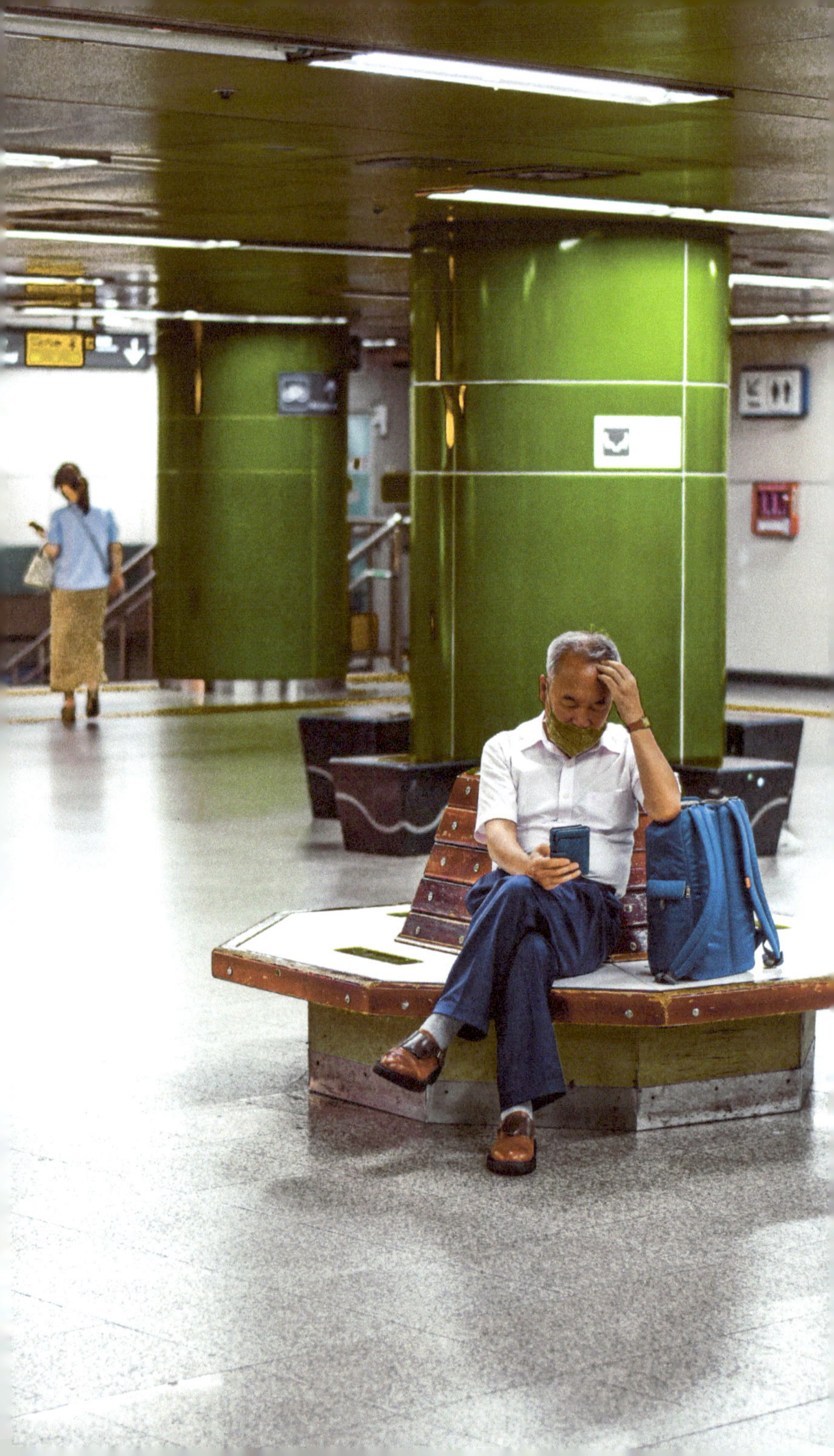

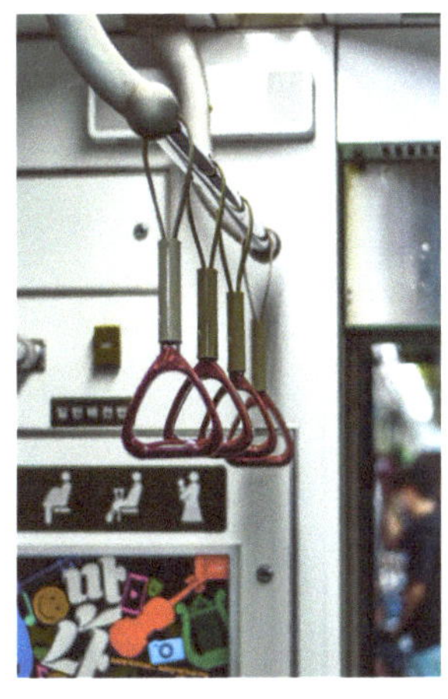

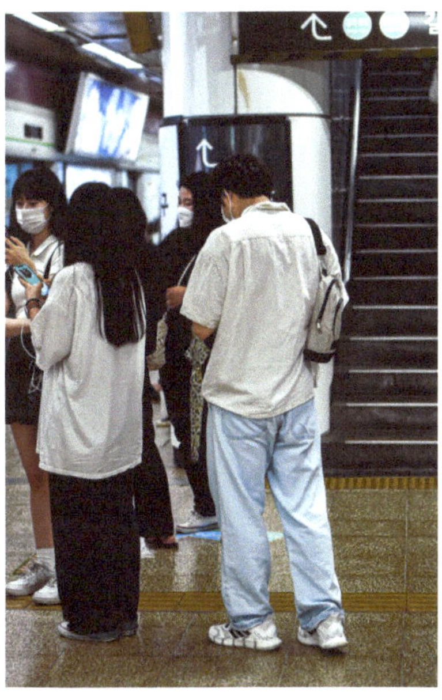

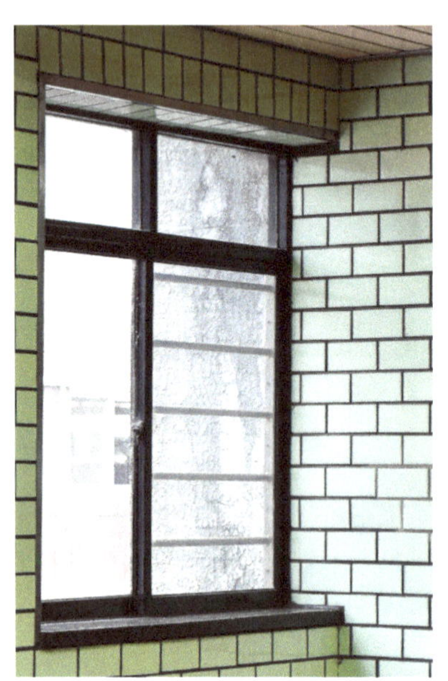

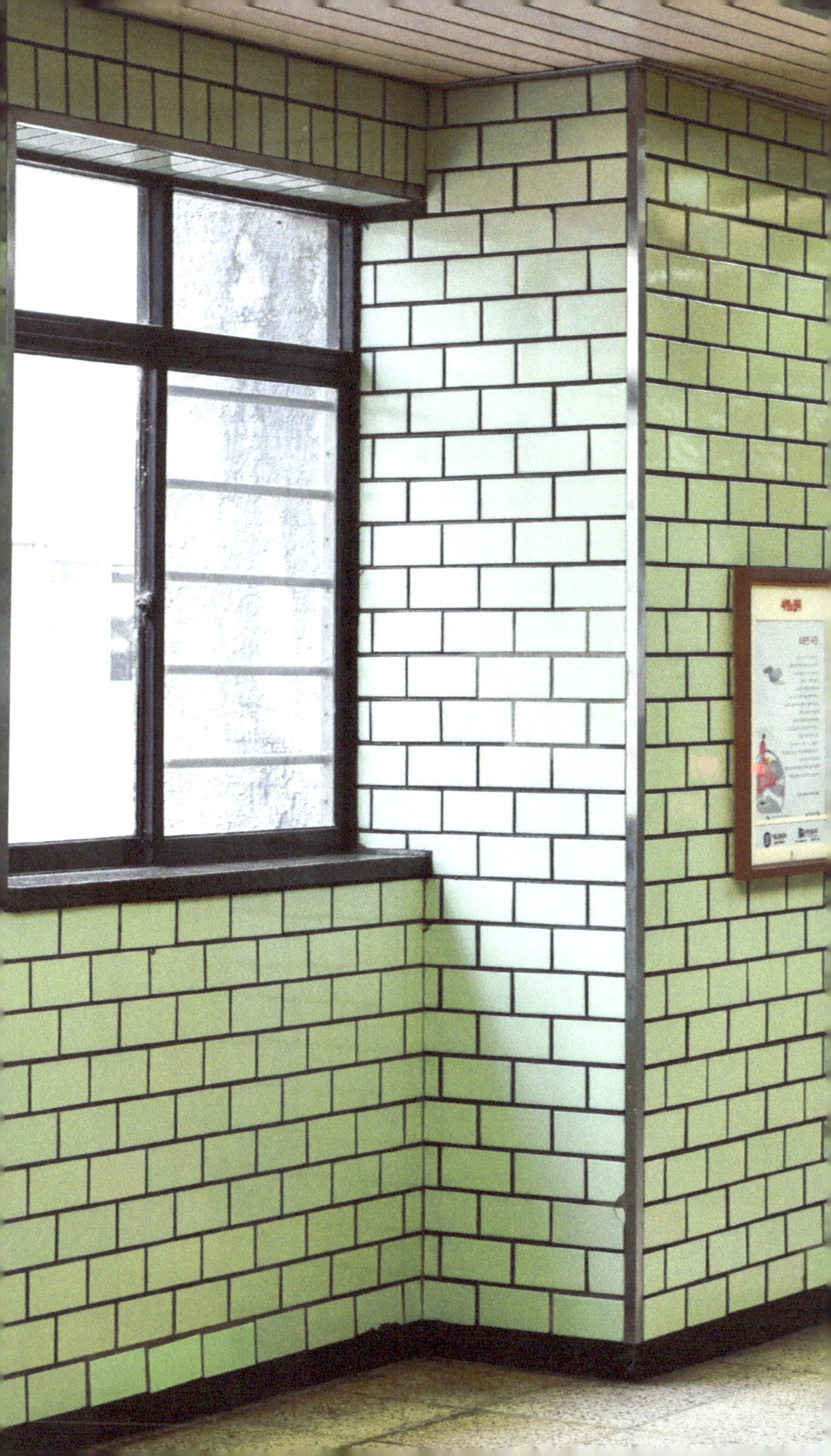

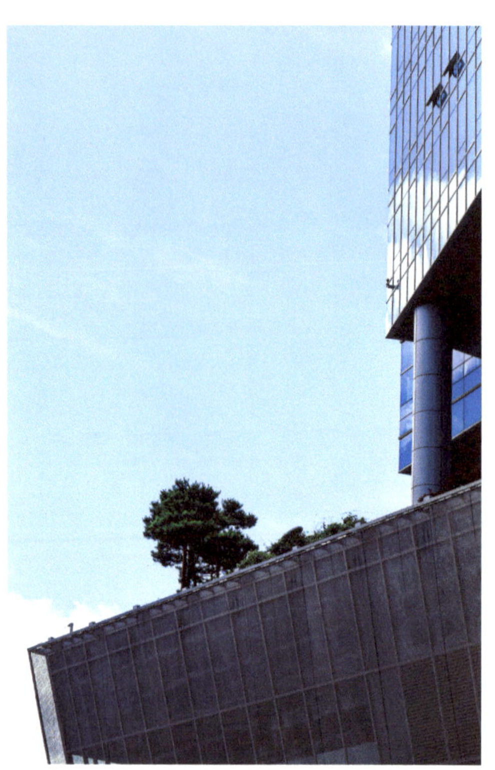

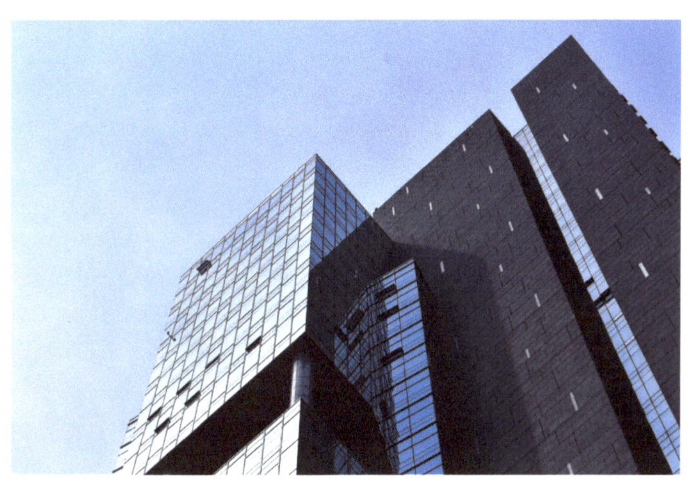

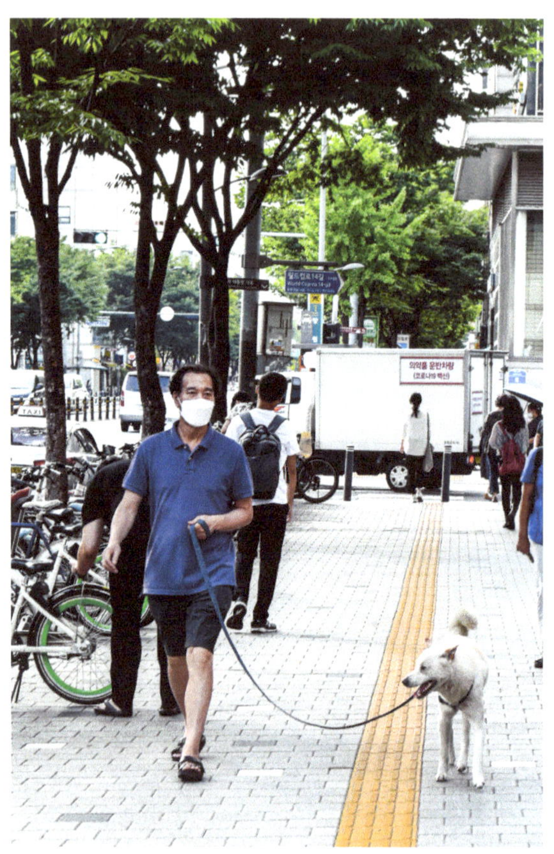
월드컵로14길
의약품 운반차량
(코로나19 백신)

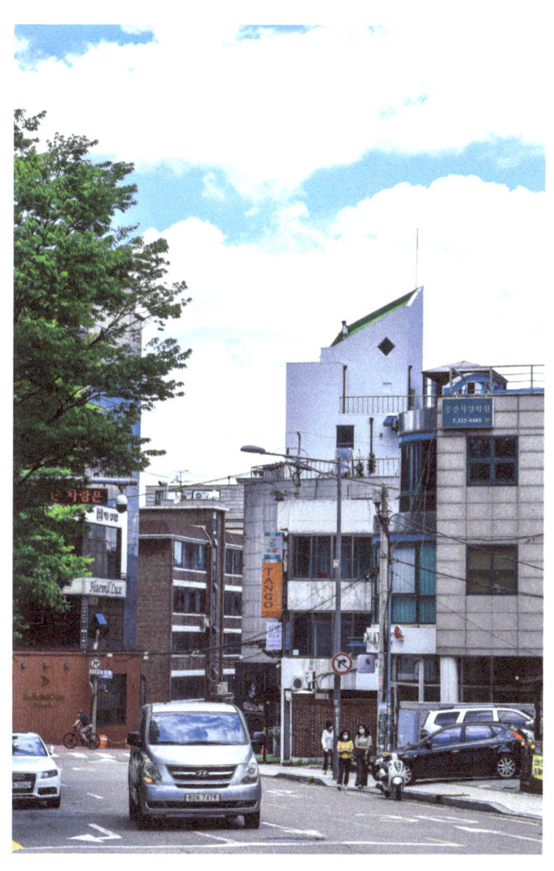
TANGO

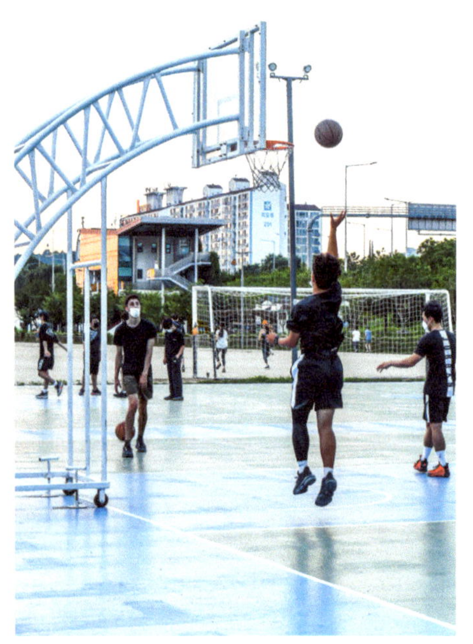

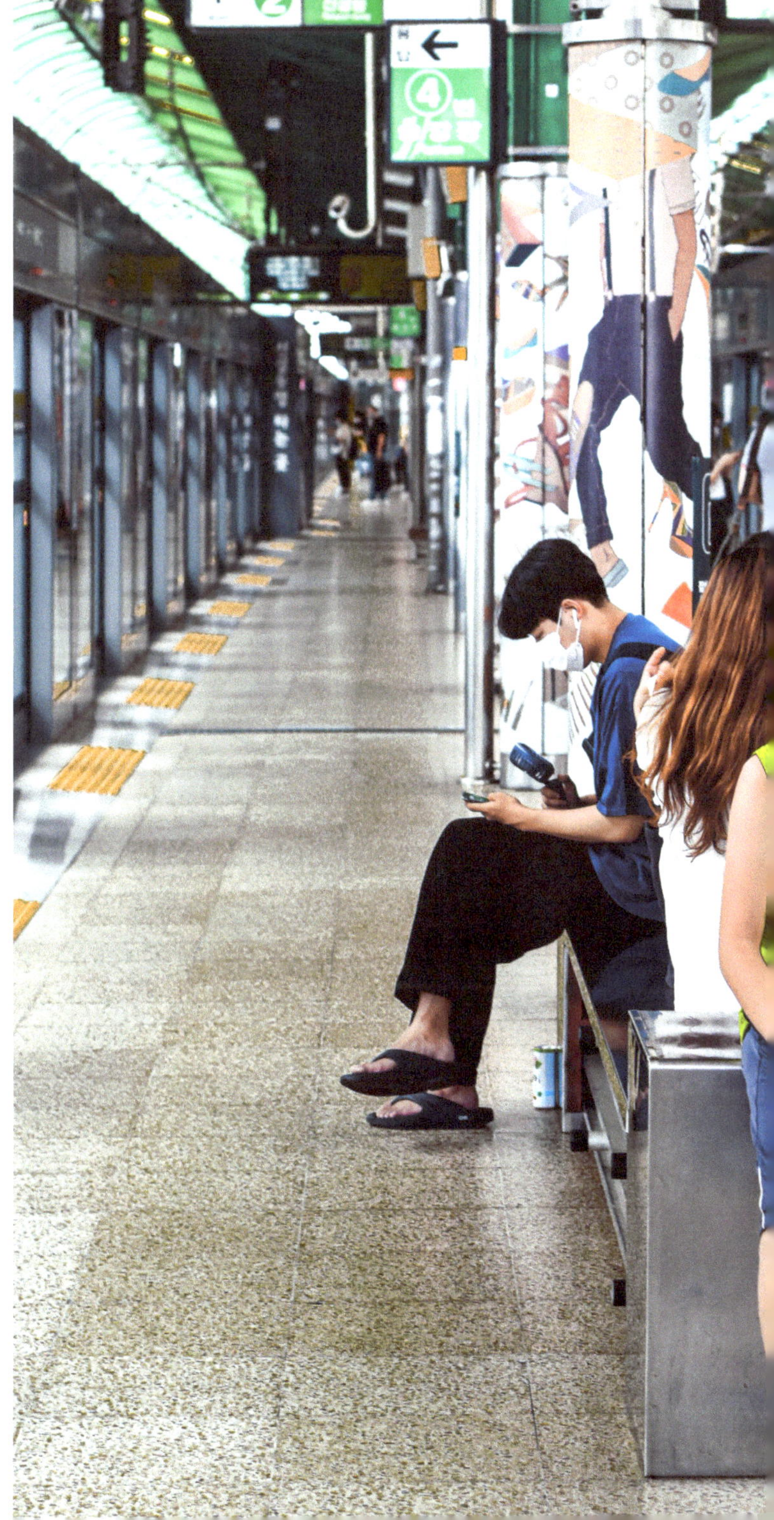

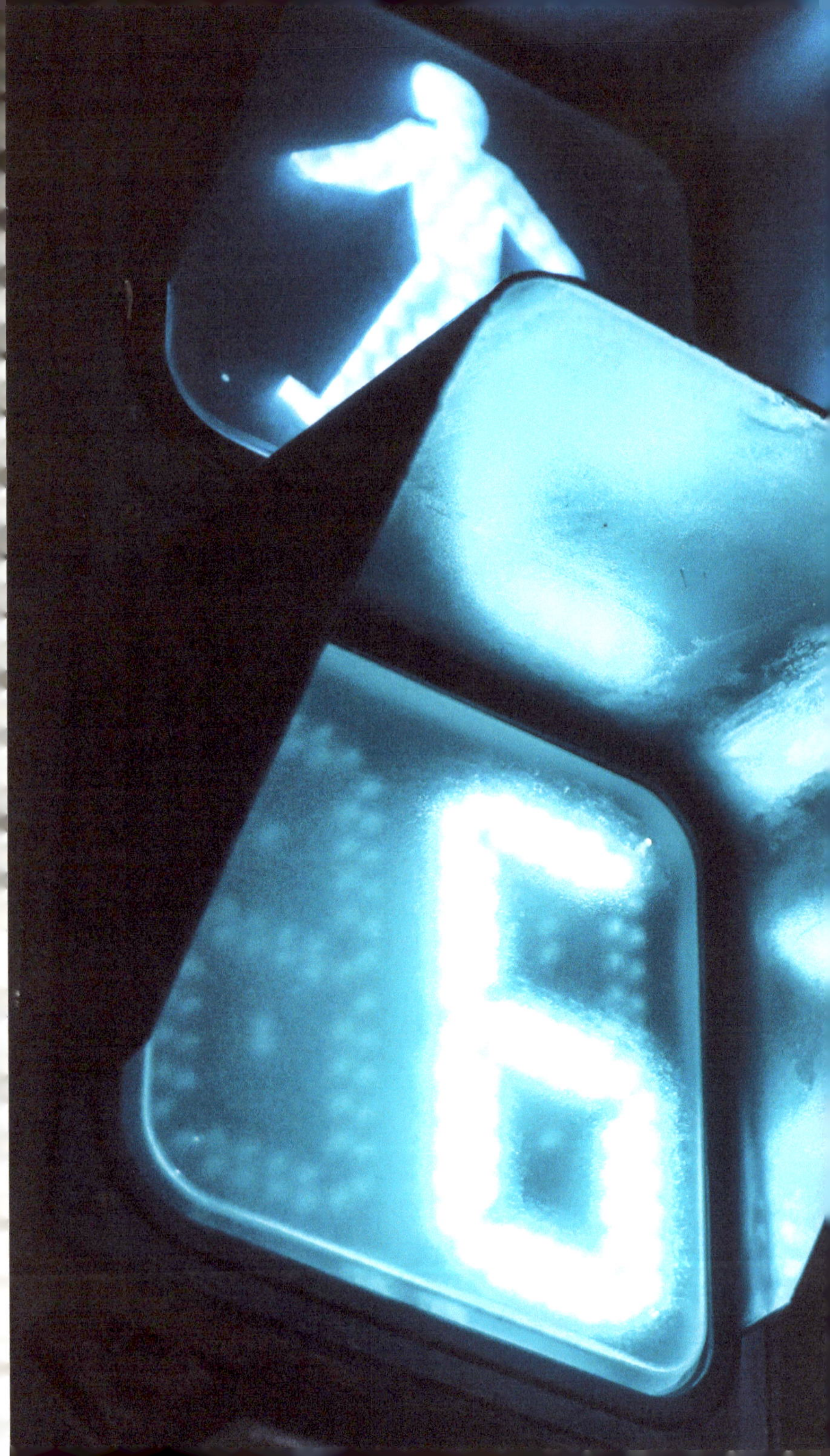
6

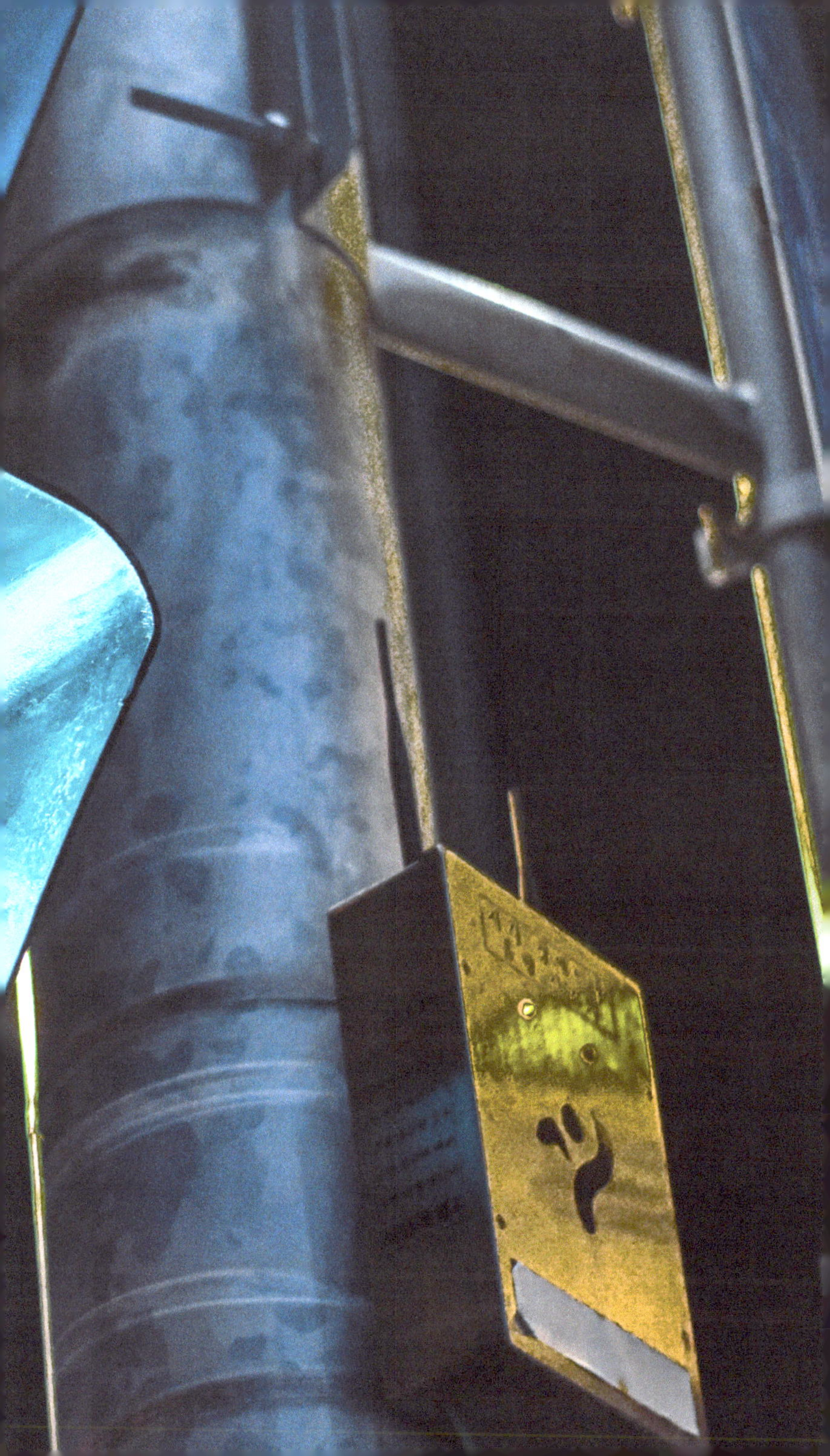

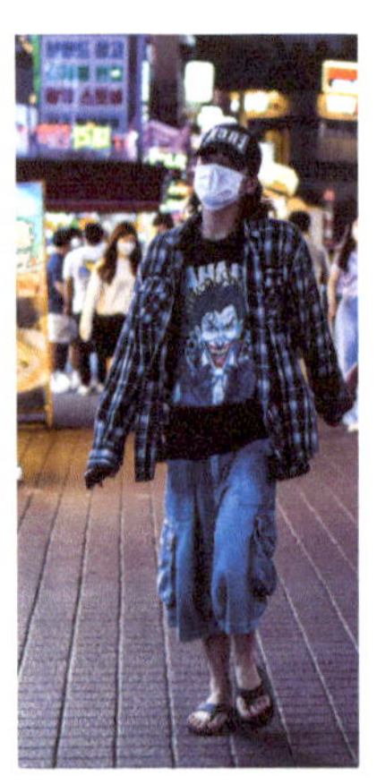

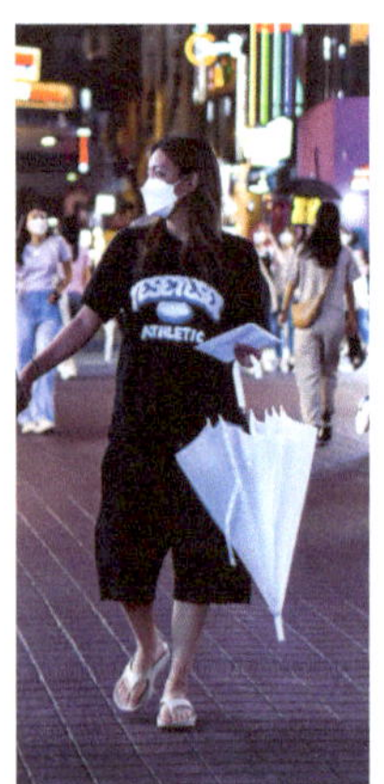

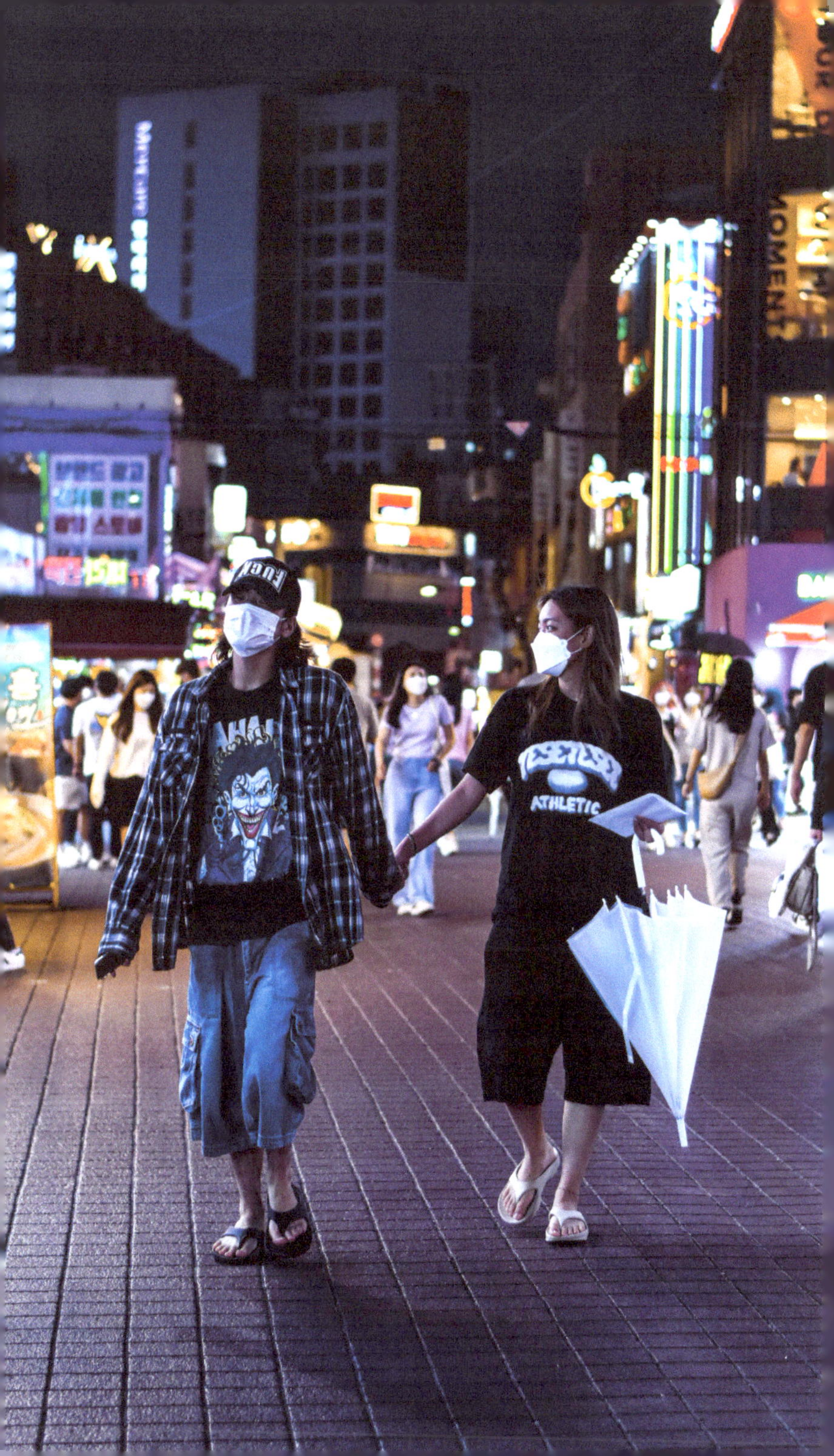
MOMENT
ATHLETIC

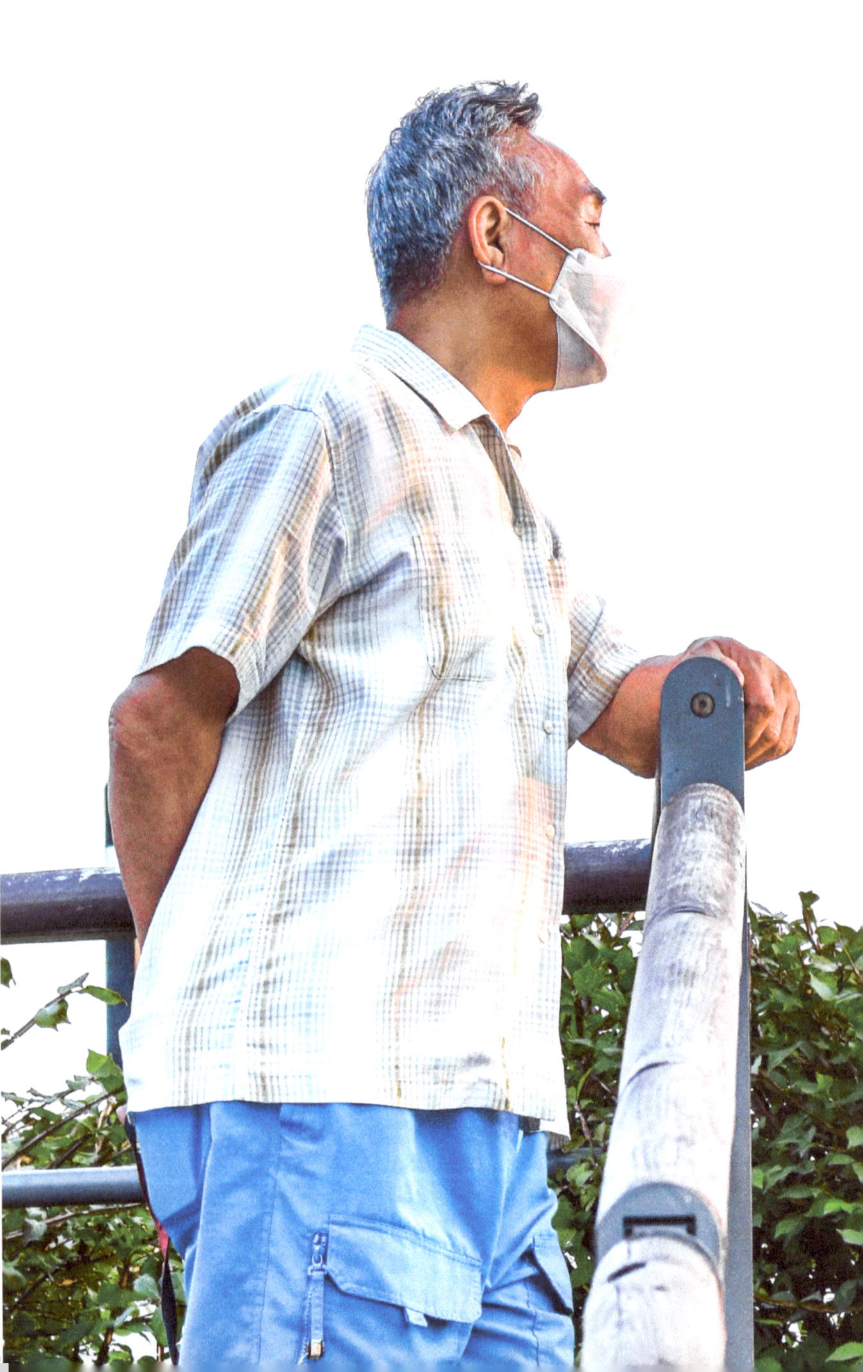

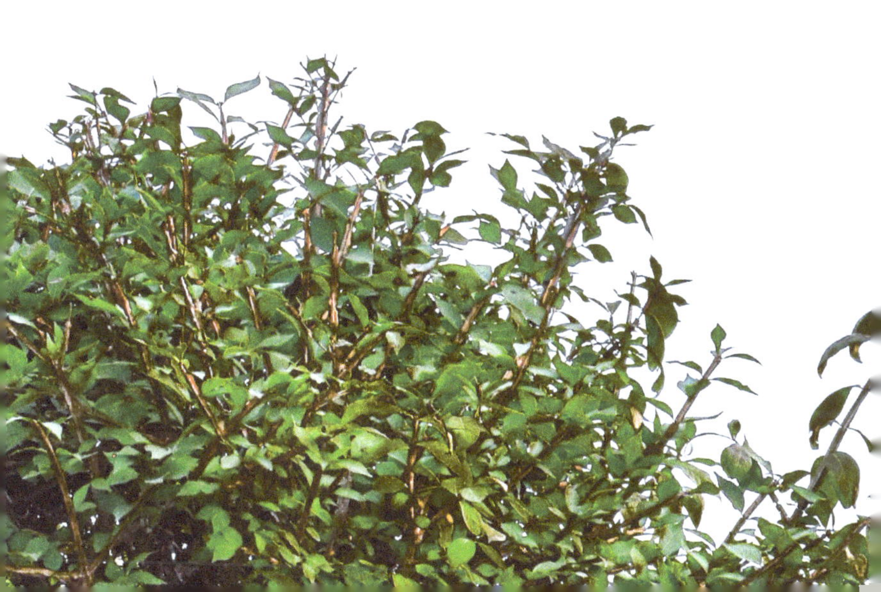

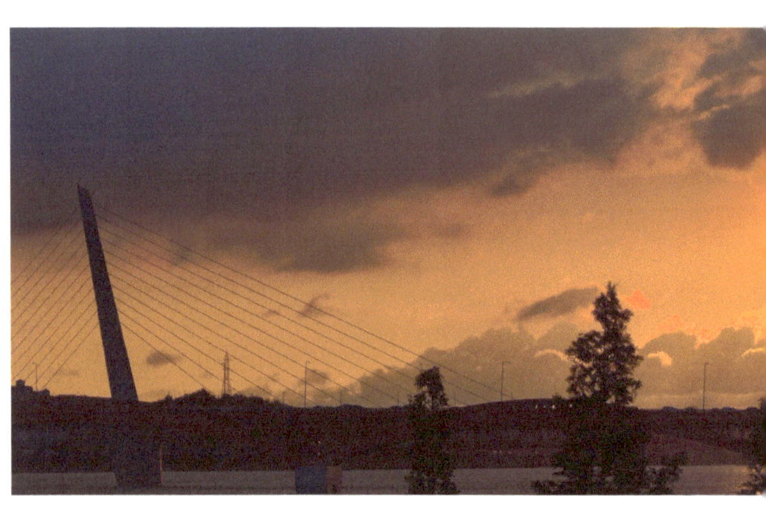

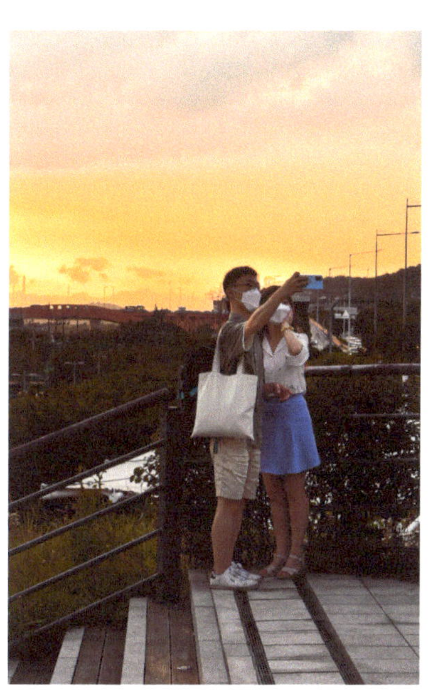

The thing about being a round-two
or round-three visitor is that you
no longer do the "touristy" things to do.
No landmarks, little to no souvenirs,
less incidents of getting lost on the subway.
It's more about the getaway,
and more about what the change in scenery
does for us humans,
to make us see and appreciate life in itself.
I know. How cliché.

The photos in this book
are in no way a well-rounded representation
of what Seoul, South Korea is.
That wasn't the point of this collection.
The point, per se, is only to document
what now feels like "art,"
as these things certainly did not feel like
they did before,
when they were surrounding me
every single day.

I suppose someday therc will be a Place C,
a place D, and a Place E. Maybe even more.
Every time another letter t is added,
new things will come to view
in each location.

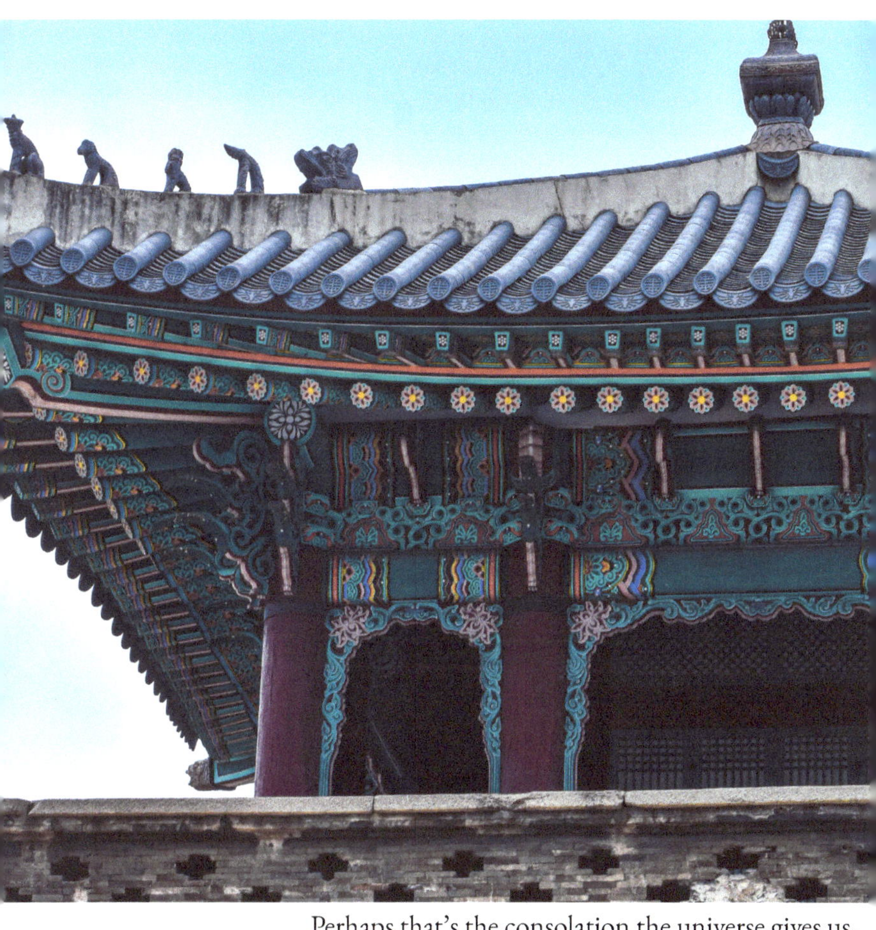

Perhaps that's the consolation the universe gives us,
to help cope with departures and goodbyes.

So as I say goodbye to my Place A for the time being,
my only hope is to return.
The next time around will be different,
as have the ones before,
and as will be the ones after.

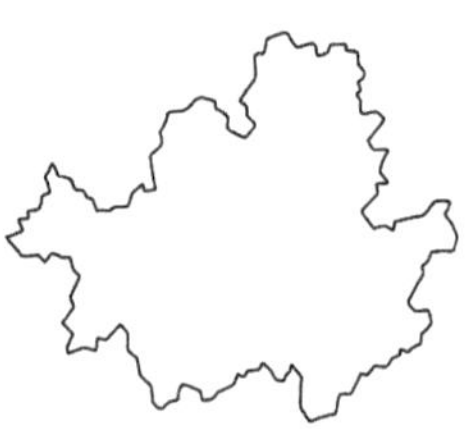

CPSIA information can be obtained
at www.ICGtesting.com
Printed in the USA
BVHW020810130921
616657BV00001B/4

* 9 7 8 1 0 8 7 9 8 2 2 6 7 *